*Verily in the*
# Remembrance of Allāh
*Do the Hearts Find Rest*

Shaykh 'Abdur-Razzāq Ibn 'Abdul-Muḥsin al-'Abbād al-Badr

**ISBN:** 978-1-6400-7442-2

**First Edition:** Rajab 1438 A.H. / April 2017 C.E.

**Cover Design:** Usul Designs

**Translation by** Mustapha Abdul Hakim Lameu Misrī

**Revision & Editing by** 'Abdullāh Omrān
abdullahomran44@live.com

**Typesetting & formatting by**
Abū Sulaymān Muḥammad 'Abdul-'Aẓīm Ibn Joshua Baker

**Printing:** Ohio Printing

**Subject:** Admonition

**Website:** www.maktabatulirshad.com
**E-mail:** info@maktabatulirshad.com

مكتبة الإرشاد
Maktabatul-Irshad
PUBLICATIONS

# BRIEF BIOGRAPHY OF THE AUTHOR

**His name:** Shaykh 'Abdur-Razzāq Ibn 'Abdul-Muḥsin al- 'Abbād al-Badr.

He is the son of the *'Allāmah* and *Muhaddith* of Madīnah Shaykh 'Abdul-Muḥsin al 'Abbād al-Badr.

**Birth:** He was born on the 22nd day of *Dhul-Qa'dah* in the year 1382 AH in az-Zal'fi, Kingdom of Saudi Arabia. He currently resides in Madīnah.

**Current Occupation:** He is a member of the teaching staff at the Islāmic University of Madīnah.

**Scholarly Certifications:** Doctorate in *'Aqīdah*.

The Shaykh has authored books, papers of research, as well as numerous explanations in different disciplines. Among them are:

1. *Fiqh of Supplications & adh-Kār.*

2. *Hajj & Refinement of Souls.*

3. Explanation of *'Exemplary Principles'* by Shaykh Ibn ʿUthaymīn (رَحِمَهُ ٱللَّهُ).

4. Explanation of the book, *The Principles of Names & Attributes*, authored by Shaykh-ul-Islām Ibn al-Qayyim (رَحِمَهُ ٱللَّهُ).

5. Explanation of the book, *Good Words*, authored by Shaykh-ul-Islām Ibn al-Qayyim (رَحِمَهُ ٱللَّهُ).

6. Explanation of the book, al- ʿAqīdah *at-Tahāwiyyah*.

7. Explanation of the book, *Fusūl: Biography of the Messenger*, by Ibn Kathīr (رَحِمَهُ ٱللَّهُ).

8. An explanation of the book, *al-Adab-ul-Mufrad*, authored by Imām Bukhārī (رَحِمَهُ ٱللَّهُ).

He studied knowledge under several scholars. The most distinguished of them are:

1. His father the *'Allāmah* Shaykh ʿAbdul-Muhsin al-Badr (حفظه الله).

2. The 'Allāmah Shaykh Ibn Bāz (رَحِمَهُ ٱللَّهُ).

3. The *'Allāmah* Shaykh Muḥammad ibn Sālih al-'Uthaymīn (رَحِمَهُ ٱللَّهُ).

4. Shaykh ʿAlī Ibn Nāsir al-Faqīhi (حفظه الله).

# TRANSLITERATION TABLE

## Consonants

| | | | | | | | |
|---|---|---|---|---|---|---|---|
| ء | ' | د | d | ض | ḍ | ك | k |
| ب | b | ذ | dh | ط | ṭ | ل | l |
| ت | t | ر | r | ظ | ẓ | م | m |
| ث | th | ز | z | ع | ' | ن | n |
| ج | j | س | s | غ | gh | هـ | h |
| ح | ḥ | ش | sh | ف | f | و | w |
| خ | kh | ص | ṣ | ق | q | ي | y |

## Vowels

| | | | | | | | |
|---|---|---|---|---|---|---|---|
| Short | َ - | a | - | i | ُ - | u | |
| Long | ـَا | ā | ـِي | ī | ـُو | ū | |

| | | | | | |
|---|---|---|---|---|---|
| Diphthongs | ـَوْ | aw | ـَيْ | ay | |

# Arabic Symbols & their meanings

|  |  |
|---|---|
| حفظه الله | May Allāh preserve him |
| رَضِوَٱللَّهُ عَنْهُ | May Allāh be pleased with him (i.e. a male companion of the Prophet Muḥammad) |
| سُبْحَانَهُ وَتَعَالَى | Glorified & Exalted is Allāh |
| عَزَّوَجَلَّ | (Allāh) the Mighty & Sublime |
| تَبَارَكَ وَتَعَالَى | (Allāh) the Blessed & Exalted |
| جَلَّ وَعَلَا | (Allāh) the Sublime & Exalted |
| عَلَيْهِ ٱلصَّلَاةُ وَٱلسَّلَامُ | May Allāh send Blessings & Safety upon him (i.e. a Prophet or Messenger) |
| صَلَّى ٱللَّهُ عَلَيْهِ وَعَلَى آلِهِ وَسَلَّمَ | May Allāh send Blessings & Safety upon him and his family (i.e. Duʿā sent when mentioning the Prophet Muḥammad) |
| رَحِمَهُ ٱللَّهُ | May Allāh have mercy on him |
| رَضِوَٱللَّهُ عَنْهُمْ | May Allāh be pleased with them (i.e. Duʿā made for the Companions of the Prophet |

Muḥammad)

جَلَّ جَلَالُهُ     (Allāh) His Majesty is Exalted

رَضِىَ اللَّهُ عَنْهَا     May Allāh be pleased with her (i.e. a female companion of the Prophet Muḥammad)

# In the Name of Allāh, the Most Gracious, the Most Merciful

All thanks and praise are due to Allāh, and prayers and blessings are upon the leader of Messengers, our Prophet Muḥammad, his family and companions.

### As for what follows:

Peace and blessings be upon you, brothers:

We will talk today about the remembrance of Allāh and what Allāh says:

**"Verily, in the remembrance of Allāh do the hearts find rest."** [*Sūrah Ar-Ra'd* 13:28]

The remembrance of Allāh has countless benefits and a great effect. Using it, hearts and souls find rest. It brings blessings and prevents evils. It makes the servant happy and successful in this worldly life and the Hereafter. The more committed the servant to remembrance, the more integrated his happiness.

When Allāh, the Almighty, says:

**"Verily, in the remembrance of Allāh do the hearts find rest."**

It means that it imparts restfulness and tranquility. When we think about this gracious verse and the reality of peoples' hearts in this worldly life, it is really complicated and filled with desires, attraction by lusts, suspicions, and seditions; leaving no place for rest in the heart save a sense of loss, displeasure, and annoyance; in short, restlessness. It means that these hearts felt restless, annoyed and lost in which one suffers from suspicions and doubts. All of it are diseases of the heart. No heart can be restful unless with the remembrance of Allāh. If it is free from the remembrance of Allāh, it is vulnerable to be infected with those illnesses. Thus, Allāh (سُبْحَانَهُ وَتَعَالَى) says:

﴿ ٱلَّذِينَ ءَامَنُواْ وَتَطْمَئِنُّ قُلُوبُهُم بِذِكْرِ ٱللَّهِ أَلَا

بِذِكْرِ ٱللَّهِ تَطْمَئِنُّ ٱلْقُلُوبُ ۝ ﴾

**"Those who believed (in the Oneness of Allāh
– Islamic Monotheism), and whose hearts find
rest in the remembrance of Allāh: Verily, in the
remembrance of Allāh do the hearts find rest."**

So, restfulness of hearts is to be happy and tranquil,
free from worries and annoyance; this can be
achieved by the remembrance of Allāh.

Without the remembrance of Allāh, the heart will die.
Abu Musa Al-Asha'ri narrated that the Prophet
(صَلَّى ٱللَّهُ عَلَيْهِ وَسَلَّمَ) said:

مَثَلُ الَّذِي يَذْكُرُ رَبَّهُ وَ الَّذِي لَا يَذْكُرُ رَبَّهُ مَثَلُ الْحَيِّ وَ الْمَيِّتِ

**"The similitude of one who remembers his
Lord and one who does not remember Him is
like that of the living and the dead."**

The Prophet (صَلَّى ٱللَّهُ عَلَيْهِ وَسَلَّمَ) gave the example of the one
who remembers Allāh with the living and the one
who does not remember Allāh with the dead; and in
another narration by Muslim, the Prophet (صَلَّى ٱللَّهُ عَلَيْهِ وَسَلَّمَ)
said:

مَثَلُ الْبَيْتِ الَّذِي يُذْكَرُ اللَّهُ فِيهِ وَالْبَيْتِ الَّذِي لَا يُذْكَرُ اللَّهُ فِيهِ مَثَلُ الْحَيِّ وَالْمَيِّتِ

"The house of which remembrance of Allāh is made and the house in which Allāh is not remembered are like the living and the dead respectively."

So, the Prophet (صَلَّى اللَّهُ عَلَيْهِ وَسَلَّمَ) gave an example of the house where Allāh is remembered with the living and the house where Allah is not remembered with the house of the dead (i.e. graves).

When we combine the words of both Ḥadīths, we find that there is a similitude of those who remember Allāh (سُبْحَانَهُ وَتَعَالَى) and fill their houses with the remembrance of Allāh (سُبْحَانَهُ وَتَعَالَى) with living ones in houses filled with life, while the ones who do not remember Allāh and no remembrance is made in their houses with the dead in the houses of the dead, as if his chest is a grave for his heart with no real life in but an animalistic one.

<u>So, hearts are divided into:</u>

❖     **A sound heart**

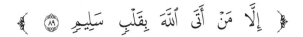

**"Except him who comes to Allāh with a sound
heart [clean from Shirk (polytheism) and Nifāq
(hypocrisy)]."** [*Sūrah Ash-Shu'arā' 26:89*]

A sound heart is a type of heart which is clean from
diseases and bad intentions. It is purified for the sake
of Allāh, and the deeds are cleaned. Thus this one
resorts to Allāh only and rely on no one but Him, and
performs acts of worship only to Allāh (سُبْحَانَهُوَتَعَالَى). If it
loves, it loves for the sake of Allāh; if it hates, it hates
for the sake of Allāh; if it supports, it supports one for
the sake of Allāh. It is a clean heart, empty from
diseases and lusts. It is closer to Allāh (سُبْحَانَهُوَتَعَالَى),
remembers Him, and worships Him only.

❖ **Second type: dead heart.** It is the heart which
turns away from his Lord and Creator and worships
others. It fails to comply with His orders, perform acts
of worship, remember Allāh, act righteous good
deeds, ask others in situations of hope, desire, and
fear, love, and hatred. It directs acts of worship and
righteous good deeds for another than Allāh. This is a
dead heart.

❖ **The third type of hearts:** the heart that features both life and death. It is charged with life when it is truthful, sincere, monotheistic, and desiring for the worship of Allāh, whereas it lacks this life when it is desires lusts and suspicions. The heart is qualified either dead or alive in pursuance with the dominant drive.

The life of the heart is sustainable when one keeps closer to Allāh and remembers Allāh (سُبْحَانَهُوَتَعَالَى) with his heart and tongue, whereby suspicions and lusts will be removed. If one does not remember Allāh, more evils and diseases shall reside.

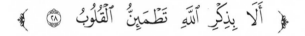

**"Verily, in the remembrance of Allāh do the hearts find rest."**

How can these hearts find rest? Through obeying Allāh, and relying upon Him and resorting to Allāh Alone. Whoever asks Allāh Alone, hopes for Allāh Alone, fears Allāh Alone, relies upon Allāh Alone, depends upon Allāh in all matters because his heart is assured with the remembrance of Allāh, for performing Tawheed and obeying Allāh (سُبْحَانَهُوَتَعَالَى).

Oh, brothers! Consider how the Prophet (ﷺ) cured who is afflicted with sadness, distress, and anxiety so we can appreciate the value of the cure that the Prophet (ﷺ) ordained by the remembrance of Allāh. All of us know that one can be afflicted with sadness, distress, and anxiety. According to the scholars, the heart can be afflicted with these diseases, one of which is related to the past (sadness), the other is related to the present time (distress), and the third is related to the future (anxiety).

*Sadness* is related to the past; one feels sad when goals are not achieved. For example, one wants to make a deal, but it fails, which causes the heart to develop a growing feeling of sadness.

*Distress* happens when one is discontent with his present situation.

If one is worried about his future, he may be anxious.

These diseases cannot be cured except with the remembrance of Allāh, and the heart cannot find rest without the assistance of Allāh. Unfortunately, brothers, when many people are afflicted with sadness, distress, and anxiety, he seeks to cure it without dependence upon Allāh or remembrance of Him. However, some people do things that incur

distress and sadness, thinking they entertain the heart
and make sadness go away. The heart cannot find
restfulness with bad deeds; only resorting to Allāh is
the proper mean to it.

How can distress, sadness, and anxiety be cured?
Consider the words of the Prophet (صَلَّى ٱللَّهُ عَلَيْهِ وَسَلَّمَ)
concerning the cure of these diseases. The Prophet
(صَلَّى ٱللَّهُ عَلَيْهِ وَسَلَّمَ) said:

مَا أَصَابَ أَحَدًا قَطُّ هَمٌّ وَلَا حَزَنٌ فَقَالَ : اللَّهُمَّ إِنِّي عَبْدُكَ وَابْنُ
عَبْدِكَ وَابْنُ أَمَتِكَ نَاصِيَتِي بِيَدِكَ مَاضٍ فِيَّ حُكْمُكَ عَدْلٌ فِيَّ
قَضَاؤُكَ أَسْأَلُكَ بِكُلِّ اسْمٍ هُوَ لَكَ سَمَّيْتَ بِهِ نَفْسَكَ أَوْ عَلَّمْتَهُ
أَحَدًا مِنْ خَلْقِكَ أَوْ أَنْزَلْتَهُ فِي كِتَابِكَ أَوْ اسْتَأْثَرْتَ بِهِ فِي عِلْمِ
الْغَيْبِ عِنْدَكَ أَنْ تَجْعَلَ الْقُرْآنَ رَبِيعَ قَلْبِي وَنُورَ صَدْرِي وَجِلَاءَ
حُزْنِي وَذَهَابَ هَمِّي إِلَّا أَذْهَبَ اللَّهُ هَمَّهُ وَحُزْنَهُ وَأَبْدَلَهُ مَكَانَهُ
فَرَجًا

**"If any Muslim is afflicted with distress and
makes this supplication, then his supplication
will be answered: O Allāh, I am Your servant,
the son of Your servant, the son of Your
maidservant. My forelock is in Your hand,
Your command concerning me prevails, and**

**Your decision concerning me is just. I call upon You by every one of the Beautiful Names by which You have described Yourself, or which You have revealed in Your Book, or You have taught to anyone of Your creatures, or which You have chosen to keep in the knowledge of the unseen with You, to make the Qurʾān the delight of my heart, the light of my chest, and to remove my sadness and dispel my anxiety." The Prophet (صَلَّىٰ ٱللَّهُ عَلَيْهِ وَسَلَّمَ) said: "If he says this, Allāh will remove his affliction and replace it with joy and happiness." They said, "O Messenger of Allāh, should we not learn it?" The Prophet (صَلَّىٰ ٱللَّهُ عَلَيْهِ وَسَلَّمَ) said: Yes, whoever hears it should know it."**

So, sadness, distress, and anxiety can be replaced by happiness.

How can this heart be happy? Saying these supplications without thinking about its meanings would be meaningless because these remembrances and supplications are worthy of deep consideration.

When one is afflicted with sadness, distress, and anxiety, he should mention starting with **"O Allāh! I am your servant."** This is a confession that he is a servant of Allāh (سُبْحَانَهُۥوَتَعَالَىٰ), who is His Creator and

Sustainer. A servant means a worshipper who obeys the orders of Allāh (سُبْحَانَهُوَتَعَالَى).

اللَّهُمَّ إني عبدك وَابْنُ عَبْدِكِ وَابْنُ أَمَتِكَ

**"O Allāh! I am your servant the son of your servant, the son of your maidservant."** I am your servant, and my father's till Adam are servants of You; all of us are servants of You and You are our Creator, Lord, and Sustainer.

نَاصِيَتِي بِيَدِكَ

**"My forelock is in your hand;"** forelock is the forehead. I do not have anything unless with Your will and Power. If You want me to live, I will live. If You want me to be happy, I will be happy. If You want me to be healthy, I will be well and healthy. If You want me to be rich, I will be rich. If You want anything else like disease, poverty, I will be ill and poor. My forelock is in Your hand, your Will and Power rule all things:

| | |
|---|---|
| وَمَـــــا شِئْتُ إِن لَمْ تَشَأْ لَمْ يكنْ | مَـــــا شِئْتَ كَانَ وإِنْ لم أَشَأْ |
| وَفِي العِلْمِ يَجري الفَتَى وَالْمُسِنْ | خَلَقْتَ العِبَادَ على مَا عَلِمْتَ |
| وهــــذا أعنتَ، وذَا لم تُعِنْ | عَلَى ذَا مَنَنْتَ، وَهَــــذا خَذلْتَ |
| وَمِنْهُمْ قَبِيحٌ، وَمِنْهُمْ حَسَنْ | فَمِنْهُمْ شَقِيٌّ، وَمِنْهُمْ سَعِيد |

VERILY IN THE REMEMBRANCE OF ALLĀH DO THE
HEARTS FIND REST

*What you want will happen even if I do not want*

*But what I want will not happen if You do not want.*

*You created people according to Your knowledge.*

*The actions of the young and the old man are consistent with Your knowledge*

*You gave, You took,*

*You support, and You forsake.*

*In the world, there are poor, happy, ugly and beautiful ones.*

نَاصِيَتِي بِيَدِكَ

**"My forelock is in your hand"** You are the Lord, the Sustainer, and I am a servant with no power but in You, as in the supplication:

لَا حَوْلَ وَ لَا قُوَّةَ إِلَّا بِاللهِ

**"There is no power but in Allāh."** No change from case to case and no power of the servant but in Allāh (سُبْحَانَهُوَتَعَالَ) so he said: **"My forelock is in your hand."**

مَاضٍ فِيَّ حُكْمُكَ

**"Your command concerning me prevails."** Your judgment will prevail with no objection because Allāh's will is sure. There is none who can reverse His judgment.

مَاضٍ فِيَّ حُكْمُكَ

**"Your command concerning me prevails"** What Allāh wills comes to pass and what He does not will not come to pass.

عَدْلٌ فِيَّ قَضَاؤُكَ

**"Your decision concerning me is just."** O Allāh! You are Just. He wrongs not, even the weight of an atom (or a small ant), and all that He judges is just.

Then one resorts to Allāh by His Beautiful Names and Great attributes.

أَسْأَلُكَ بِكُلِّ اسْمٍ هُوَ لَكَ

**"I call upon You by every one of the Beautiful Names by which You have described Yourself."** Meaning: O Allāh! I call upon You with all Your Names. It is known that the best way to call upon

Allāh is by His Names and Attributes. Allāh
(سُبْحَانَهُوَتَعَالَى) says:

$$﴿ وَلِلَّهِ ٱلْأَسْمَآءُ ٱلْحُسْنَىٰ فَٱدْعُوهُ بِهَا ﴾$$

"And (all) the Most Beautiful Names belong to
Allāh, so call on Him by them." [*Sūrah Al-A'rāf*
7:180]

And Allāh (سُبْحَانَهُوَتَعَالَى) says:

$$﴿ قُلِ ٱدْعُواْ ٱللَّهَ أَوِ ٱدْعُواْ ٱلرَّحْمَٰنَ أَيَّا مَّا تَدْعُواْ$$
$$فَلَهُ ٱلْأَسْمَآءُ ٱلْحُسْنَىٰ ﴾$$

"Say (O Muḥammad (صَلَّىٱللَّهُعَلَيْهِوَسَلَّمَ)): "Invoke
Allāh or invoke the Most Gracious (Allāh), by
whatever name you invoke Him (it is the
same), for to Him belong the Best Names."
[*Sūrah Al-Isra'* 17:110]

And Allāh (سُبْحَانَهُوَتَعَالَى) says:

$$﴿ ٱللَّهُ لَآ إِلَٰهَ إِلَّا هُوَ لَهُ ٱلْأَسْمَآءُ ٱلْحُسْنَىٰ ۝﴾$$

**"Allāh! La ilaha illa Huwa (none has the right to be worshiped but He)! To Him belong the Best Names."** [*Sūrah Taha* 21:8]

and Allāh (سُبْحَانَهُوَتَعَالَ) says:

﴿ هُوَ ٱللَّهُ ٱلَّذِى لَآ إِلَهَ إِلَّا هُوَ عَلِمُ ٱلْغَيْبِ وَٱلشَّهَدَةِ هُوَ ٱلرَّحْمَنُ ٱلرَّحِيمُ ۝ هُوَ ٱللَّهُ ٱلَّذِى لَآ إِلَهَ إِلَّا هُوَ ٱلْمَلِكُ ٱلْقُدُّوسُ ٱلسَّلَمُ ٱلْمُؤْمِنُ ٱلْمُهَيْمِنُ ٱلْعَزِيزُ ٱلْجَبَّارُ ٱلْمُتَكَبِّرُ سُبْحَنَ ٱللَّهِ عَمَّا يُشْرِكُونَ ۝ هُوَ ٱللَّهُ ٱلْخَلِقُ ٱلْبَارِئُ ٱلْمُصَوِّرُ لَهُ ٱلْأَسْمَآءُ ٱلْحُسْنَىٰ يُسَبِّحُ لَهُ مَا فِى ٱلسَّمَوَتِ وَٱلْأَرْضِ وَهُوَ ٱلْعَزِيزُ ٱلْحَكِيمُ ۝ ﴾

**"He is Allāh, beside Whom La ilaha illa Huwa (none has the right to be worshiped but He) the All-Knower of the unseen and the seen. He is the Most Gracious, the Most Merciful. He is Allāh beside Whom La ilaha illa Huwa (none has the right to be worshiped but He), the King, the Holy, the One Free from all defects,**

the Giver of security, the Watcher over His creatures, the All-Mighty, the Compeller, the Supreme. Glorified is Allāh! (High is He) Above all that they associate as partners with Him. He is Allāh, the Creator, the Inventor of all things, the Bestower of forms. To Him belong the Best Names. All that is in the heavens and the earth glorify Him. And He is the All-Mighty, the All-Wise." [*Sūrah Al-Hashr* 59:22-24]

So, the servant calls upon Allāh with His Most Beautiful Names.

أَسْأَلُكَ بِكُلِّ اسْمٍ هُوَ لَكَ سَمَّيْتَ بِهِ نَفْسَكَ أَوْ عَلَّمْتَهُ أَحَدًا مِنْ خَلْقِكَ أَوْ أَنْزَلْتَهُ فِي كِتَابِكَ أَوِ اسْتَأْثَرْتَ بِهِ فِي عِلْمِ الْغَيْبِ عِنْدَكَ

"I call upon You by every one of the Beautiful Names by which You have described Yourself, or which You have revealed in Your Book, or You have taught to anyone of Your creatures, or which You have chosen to keep in the knowledge of the unseen with You."

I call upon You with all Your Beautiful Names.

Then he requests,

أَنْ تَجْعَلَ الْقُرْآنَ رَبِيعَ قَلْبِي

**"To make the Qur'ān the delight of my heart."**

What is in his heart? In his heart, there is sadness and distress that make him sick, so he wants to remove it by these ways, and then called upon Allāh, **"to make the Qur'ān the delight of my heart"** to make me busy with the Qur'ān, to make my heart full of the Qur'ān. When the heart is occupied with the Qur'ān, there will be no sadness, no distress, no anxiety because there is no place for these diseases. Sadness, distress, and anxiety cannot find a way to his heart as it is full of the remembrance of Allāh.

أَنْ تَجْعَلَ الْقُرْآنَ رَبِيعَ قَلْبِي وَنُورَ صَدْرِي

**"To make the Qur'ān the spring of my heart, the light of my chest."**

Consider that when the heart is mentioned, he said **"the spring of my heart"** and when the chest is mentioned he said: **"the light of my chest."**

Thus, he mentioned the spring and the light. The spring refers to nutrition, plants, life and increase. It is known that is the life of the human body and setting it right arise from the heart. Also, growth and life of plants and trees are from its origin, thus when the heart is set right, the body will be right. So, he said:

أَنْ تَجْعَلَ الْقُرْآنَ رَبِيعَ قَلْبِي

**"to make the Qurʾān the spring of my heart."**

Meaning: make it nourish the heart, like water that feeds plants. You know how the plant will be if it is not irrigated with water? It will die, but if it is watered, it will bloom. Allāh (سُبْحَانَهُوَتَعَالَى) says:

۞ أَلَمْ يَأْنِ لِلَّذِينَ ءَامَنُوٓاْ أَن تَخْشَعَ قُلُوبُهُمْ لِذِكْرِ ٱللَّهِ وَمَا نَزَلَ مِنَ ٱلْحَقِّ وَلَا يَكُونُواْ كَٱلَّذِينَ أُوتُواْ ٱلْكِتَٰبَ مِن قَبْلُ فَطَالَ عَلَيْهِمُ ٱلْأَمَدُ فَقَسَتْ قُلُوبُهُمْ وَكَثِيرٌ مِّنْهُمْ فَٰسِقُونَ ۝ ٱعْلَمُوٓاْ أَنَّ ٱللَّهَ يُحْيِ ٱلْأَرْضَ بَعْدَ مَوْتِهَا قَدْ بَيَّنَّا لَكُمُ ٱلْءَايَٰتِ لَعَلَّكُمْ تَعْقِلُونَ ۝

**"Has not the time come for the hearts of those who believe (in the Oneness of Allāh – Islamic Monotheism) to be affected by Allāh's**

Reminder (this Qur'ān), and that which has been revealed of the truth, lest they become as those who received the Scripture [the Taurat (Torah) and the Injeel (Gospel)] before (i.e. Jews and Christians), and the term was prolonged for them and so their hearts were hardened? And many of them were Fāsiqūn (the rebellious, the disobedient to Allāh). Know that Allāh gives life to the earth after its death! Indeed, We have made clear the Ayat (proofs, evidence, verses, lessons, signs, revelations, etc.) to you if you but understand."
[*Sūrah Al-Hadid* 57:16-17]

Allāh (سُبْحَانَهُوَتَعَالَى) called the Qur'ān *Rūh* (Revelation) in many verses in the Qur'ān as Allāh (سُبْحَانَهُوَتَعَالَى) says:

﴿ أَتَىٰٓ أَمْرُ ٱللَّهِ فَلَا تَسْتَعْجِلُوهُۚ سُبْحَٰنَهُۥ وَتَعَٰلَىٰ عَمَّا يُشْرِكُونَ ۝ يُنَزِّلُ ٱلْمَلَٰٓئِكَةَ بِٱلرُّوحِ مِنْ أَمْرِهِۦ عَلَىٰ مَن يَشَآءُ مِنْ عِبَادِهِۦٓ أَنْ أَنذِرُوٓاْ أَنَّهُۥ لَآ إِلَٰهَ إِلَّآ أَنَا۠ فَٱتَّقُونِ ۝ ﴾

"The Commandment (the Hour or the punishment of the disbelievers and polytheists or the Islamic laws or commandments)

ordained by Allāh will come to pass, so, seek
not to hasten it. Glorified and Exalted is He
above all that they associate as partners with
Him. He sends down the angels with the Ruh
(revelation) of His Command to whom of His
slaves He wills (saying): "Warn (mankind) that
La ilaha illa Ana (none has the right to be
worshipped but I), so fear Me (by abstaining
from sins and evil deeds)." [*Sūrah An-Nahl* 16:
1-2]

In another verse, Allāh (سُبْحَانَهُوَتَعَالَى) says:

$$﴿ وَكَذَٰلِكَ أَوْحَيْنَا إِلَيْكَ رُوحًا مِّنْ أَمْرِنَا ﴾$$

"And thus, We have sent to you (O
Muḥammad (صَلَّىٱللَّهُعَلَيْهِوَسَلَّمَ)) Rūh (a Revelation,
and a Mercy) of Our Command."

And,

$$﴿ وَكَذَٰلِكَ أَوْحَيْنَا إِلَيْكَ رُوحًا مِّنْ أَمْرِنَا مَا كُنتَ
تَدْرِى مَا ٱلْكِتَبُ وَلَا ٱلْإِيمَنُ وَلَٰكِن جَعَلْنَهُ نُورًا
نَّهْدِى بِهِۦ مَن نَّشَآءُ مِنْ عِبَادِنَا وَإِنَّكَ لَتَهْدِىٓ إِلَىٰ
صِرَٰطٍ مُّسْتَقِيمٍ ۝ ﴾$$

"And thus, We have sent to you (O
Muḥammad (ﷺ)) Rūh (a Revelation,
and a Mercy) of Our Command. You knew not
what is the Book, nor what is Faith? But We
have made it (this Qur'ān) a light wherewith
We guide whosoever of Our Slaves We will.
And verily, you (O Muḥammad (ﷺ)) are
indeed guiding (mankind) to a Straight Path
(i.e. Allāh's Religion of Islāmic Monotheism)."
[Sūrah Ash-Shura 42:52]

So, the Qur'ān is a life for the heart. In this Ḥadīth,
one calls upon Allāh to fill his heart with the Qur'ān
and remembrance of Allāh so as to remove the
diseases in the heart.

"The light of my chest;" make a light in my chest by
caring and keeping the Noble Qur'ān. This indicates
that the Qur'ān and the remembrance of Allāh make
the heart full of light.

O' brothers! How can sadness, distress, and anxiety
affect a heart the Qur'ān is its spring and light?
However, weakness of faith affects a man badly so his
heart may be afflicted with those diseases, which will
cause the heart to become restless, suspicious and
bored.

أَنْ تَجْعَلَ الْقُرْآنَ الْعَظِيمَ رَبِيعَ قَلْبِي وَ نُورَ صَدْرِي وَجِلَاءَ حُزْنِي

**"To make the Qur'ān the delight of my heart, the light of my chest, and to remove my sadness and dispel my anxiety."** One asks Allah to remove sadness from the heart and to dispel the anxiety.

The Prophet (ﷺ) said:

إِلَّا أَذْهَبَ اللهُ هَمَّهُ وَ غَمَّهُ وَ أَبْدَلَهُ فَرحاً

**"Allāh will remove his affliction and replace it with joy and happiness."**

When the companions heard this Ḥadīth, they asked the Prophet (ﷺ):

يَا رَسُولَ اللَّهِ أَلَا نَتَعَلَّمُهَا ؟ -هذا الدعاء ألا نتعلمه - قال: ((بَلَى يَنْبَغِي لِمَنْ سَمِعَهَا أَنْ يَتَعَلَّمَهَا))

**"O Messenger of Allāh, should we not learn it?" The Prophet (ﷺ) said: Yes, whoever hears it should know it."**

It is a great supplication in which one can find the remembrance of Allāh (سُبْحَانَهُوَتَعَالَى) and resorting to Allāh.

So, we learned from this great Ḥadīth the value of the remembrance of Allāh and how it affects the heart concerning achieving restfulness and tranquility, in addition to removal of sadness, distress, and anxiety.

In this regard, we should not forget about the causes of restlessness of the heart. Thus, whoever wants his heart to be restful, he needs to attend to this matter; to be cautious of the causes that impact discomfort.

Allāh (سُبْحَانَهُوَتَعَالَى) says that there is an enemy who sees us, but we do not see, and it circulates in the human body as blood does. Also, this enemy is a dangerous one who does his best to keep one away from Allāh's obedience, and he is so malicious. This enemy relentlessly plots to turn people away from the Allāh's Path, with a long experience in doing so. Many people are caused to enter the graves upon deviance.

﴿ وَمَا يُؤْمِنُ أَكْثَرُهُم بِٱللَّهِ إِلَّا وَهُم مُّشْرِكُونَ ۝ ﴾

**"And most of them believe not in Allāh except that they attribute partners to Him [i.e. they are Mushrikūn i.e. polytheists.]"** [*Sūrah Yusuf* 12:106]

And,

﴿ وَمَآ أَكْثَرُ ٱلنَّاسِ وَلَوْ حَرَصْتَ بِمُؤْمِنِينَ ۝ ﴾

**"And most of mankind will not believe even if
you desire it eagerly."** [*Sūrah Yusuf* 12: 103]

Many people are deceived by Shayṭān who turned
them away from what they are created for. Allāh
(سُبْحَانَهُوَتَعَالَى) warned us of this enemy and said:

﴿ إِنَّ ٱلشَّيْطَنَ لَكُمْ عَدُوٌّ فَٱتَّخِذُوهُ عَدُوًّا ﴾

**"Surely, Shayṭān is an enemy to you, so take
(treat) him as an enemy."** [*Sūrah Fatir* 35:6]

Allāh (سُبْحَانَهُوَتَعَالَى) says that this enemy will come to
them from before them and behind them, from their
right and their left, from all sides,

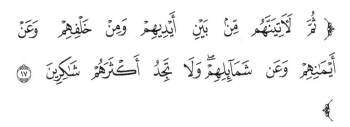

**"Then I will come to them before them and
behind them, from their right and their left,**

**and You will not find most of them as thankful ones (i.e. they will not be dutiful to You)."** [Sūrah Al-A'rāf 7:17]

This enemy made many plans and used many ways to turn the heart away from the remembrance of Allāh so that restfulness will go away. Allāh (سُبْحَانَهُوَتَعَالَى) said:

$$﴿ وَمَن يَعْشُ عَن ذِكْرِ ٱلرَّحْمَٰنِ نُقَيِّضْ لَهُۥ شَيْطَٰنًا فَهُوَ لَهُۥ قَرِينٌ ۝ ﴾$$

**"And whosoever turns away blindly from the remembrance of the Most Gracious (Allāh) (i.e. this Qur'ān and worship of Allāh), We appoint for him a Shaytān to be a Qarin (a companion) to him."** [Sūrah az-Zukhruf 43:36]

So, Shaytān enters one's heart when he turns away from the remembrance of Allāh. The more one's heart is turning away from the remembrance of Allāh (سُبْحَانَهُوَتَعَالَى), the more the Shaytān will consume one's, heart. No way to prevent oneself from this Shaytān but by the remembrance of Allāh.

Thus, the Hadīth related in Al-Musnad concerning the story of Allāh's order to Yahya ibn Zakarīyā (عَلَيْهِمَاٱلسَّلَامُ)

with five commandments to abide by, and to command the Children of Israel to abide by them.

وَآمُرُكُمْ بِذِكْرِ اللَّهِ عَزَّ وَجَلَّ كَثِيرًا ، وَإِنَّ مَثَلَ ذَلِكَ كَمَثَلِ رَجُلٍ طَلَبَهُ الْعَدُوُّ سِرَاعًا فِي أَثَرِهِ فَأَتَى حِصْنًا حَصِينًا فَتَحَصَّنَ فِيهِ ، وَإِنَّ الْعَبْدَ أَحْصَنُ مَا يَكُونُ مِنَ الشَّيْطَانِ إِذَا كَانَ فِي ذِكْرِ اللَّهِ عَزَّ وَجَلَّ

**And He commands you to remember Allāh. For indeed the parable of that is a man whose enemy quickly tracks him until he reaches an impermeable fortress in which he protects himself from them. This is how the worshipper is; he does not protect himself from Shayṭān except by the remembrance of Allāh."**

This is an example of who remembers Allāh (سُبْحَانَهُ وَتَعَالَى) as a man who entered a fortress to protect himself from the enemy. Many scholars used the word 'fortress' to name their books concerning the remembrance of Allāh, because the Muslim protects himself, his heart, his home by the remembrance of Allāh (سُبْحَانَهُ وَتَعَالَى).

It is narrated in the Ḥadīth that if one entered his house without saying "in the name of Allāh," the Shayṭān say, 'You have found a place to stay the night, and if he started eating without saying, "in the name of Allāh," Shayṭān says, 'you have found food.' This indicates that if one is committed to the remembrance of Allāh when entering and leaving the house, drinking and eating, mounting and dismounting, and all other cases, Shayṭān cannot find a way to his heart. This is the meaning of what Allāh (سُبْحَانَهُوَتَعَالَى) says:

$$﴿ وَمَن يَعْشُ عَن ذِكْرِ ٱلرَّحْمَٰنِ نُقَيِّضْ لَهُۥ شَيْطَٰنًا فَهُوَ لَهُۥ قَرِينٌ ۝ ﴾$$

"And whosoever turns away blindly from the remembrance of the Most Gracious (Allāh) (i.e. this Qur'ān and worship of Allāh), We appoint for him (Shayṭān) to be a Qarin (a companion) to him." [Sūrah az-Zukhruf 43:36]

The Prophet (صَلَّىٱللَّهُعَلَيْهِوَسَلَّمَ) said:

$$إِنَّ الشَّيْطَانَ لَا يَدْخُلُ بَيْتًا تُقْرَأُ فِيهِ سُورَةُ الْبَقَرَةِ$$

"Shayṭān doesn't enter the house in which Sūrah Baqarah is recited."

It is related in the Ḥadīth that whoever recited Ayatul-Kursi at night, then, no Shayṭān shall come near him till the morning, and Allāh will protect him. Also, it is related that if one intends to have sexual intercourse with his wife, he should say:

بسم الله اللّٰهُمَّ جنِّبنا الشيطان وجنِّب الشيطان ما رزقتنا ثم كُتب له ولد لا يقربه شيطان

**"In the Name of Allāh, O Allāh! Keep us away from Shayṭān and keep Shayṭān away from what You have bestowed upon us;" and if Allāh has ordained a child for them, Shayṭān will never harm him."**

These are fortifications and supplications to protect them from Shayṭān.

Furthermore, it is related that,

مَنْ قَرَأَ بِالْآيَتَيْنِ مِنْ آخِرِ سُورَةِ الْبَقَرَةِ فِي لَيْلَةٍ كَفَتَاهُ

**"He who recites the two verses at the end of Surat Al-Baqarah at night, they will suffice him."**

It will protect him by seeking refuge with Allāh (سُبْحَانَهُوَتَعَالَى) from the enemy.

﴿ وَإِمَّا يَنزَغَنَّكَ مِنَ ٱلشَّيْطَانِ نَزْغٌ فَٱسْتَعِذْ
بِٱللَّهِ إِنَّهُ هُوَ ٱلسَّمِيعُ ٱلْعَلِيمُ ۝ ﴾

"And if an evil whisper from Shayṭān
(Shayṭān) tries to turn you away (from doing
good), then seek refuge in Allāh. Verily, He is
the All-Hearer, the All-Knower." [Sūrah Fussilat
41:36]

And,

﴿ وَقُل رَّبِّ أَعُوذُ بِكَ مِنْ هَمَزَاتِ ٱلشَّيَاطِينِ
۝ وَأَعُوذُ بِكَ رَبِّ أَن يَحْضُرُونِ ۝ ﴾

"And say: "My Lord! I seek refuge with You
from the whisperings (suggestions) of the
Shayatin (plural of Shayṭān). And I seek
refuge with You, My Lord! lest they should
come near me." [Sūrah Al-Mu'minun 23:97-98]

And,

﴿ قُلْ أَعُوذُ بِرَبِّ ٱلنَّاسِ ۝ مَلِكِ
ٱلنَّاسِ ۝ إِلَهِ ٱلنَّاسِ ۝ مِن شَرِّ

ٱلْوَسْوَاسِ ٱلْخَنَّاسِ ۝ ٱلَّذِى يُوَسْوِسُ فِى
صُدُورِ ٱلنَّاسِ ۝ مِنَ ٱلْجِنَّةِ وَٱلنَّاسِ
۝

"Say: "I seek refuge with (Allāh) the Lord of mankind, The King of mankind – The Ilah (God) of mankind, From the evil of the whisperer (Shayṭān who whispers evil in the hearts of men) who withdraws (from his whispering in one's heart after one remembers Allāh). Who whispers in the breasts of mankind; of Jinn and men." [*Sūrah An-Nās* 114:1-6]

Ibn Abbas (رَضِيَٱللَّهُعَنْهُمَا) said pertaining the meaning of (whisperer who withdraws):

هذا الشيطان إذا غفل الإنسان عن ذكر الله وسوس - يعني
الشيطان - وسوس للإنسان ، فإذا ذكر الإنسان الله خنس -
- يعني ذهب وابتعد -

*"This is the Shayṭān when one turns away from the remembrance of Allāh, Shayṭān will whisper, but when Allāh is remembered, Shayṭān will withdraw."*

SHAYKH 'ABDUR-RAZZĀQ IBN 'ABDUL-MUḤSIN AL-'ABBĀD AL-BADR

Thus, one needs always to remember Allāh so that the Shayṭān withdraws and turns away from him. However, if one continues keeping away from the remembrance of Allāh, Shayṭān will enter his heart. So, one needs to draw closer to Allāh (سُبْحَانَهُوَتَعَالَى), rely upon Him, resort to Him. Thus Shayṭān will be driven away.

$$﴿ وَمَن يَعْتَصِم بِاللَّهِ فَقَدْ هُدِىَ إِلَى صِرَاطٍ مُّسْتَقِيمٍ ۝ ﴾$$

"And whoever holds firmly to Allāh, (i.e. follows Islam – Allāh's religion, and practically obeys all that Allāh has ordered), then he is indeed guided to a Right Path." [*Sūrah Al-Imran*3:101]

The Prophet (صَلَّ ٱللَّهُعَلَيْهِوَسَلَّمَ) was saying in his supplication – in the morning, afternoon and when sleeping:

اللَّهُمَّ فَاطِرَ السَّمَوَاتِ وَالْأَرْضِ عَالِمَ الْغَيْبِ وَالشَّهَادَةِ لَا إِلَهَ إِلَّا أَنْتَ رَبَّ كُلِّ شَيْءٍ وَمَلِيكَهُ أَعُوذُ بِكَ مِنْ شَرِّ نَفْسِي وَمِنْ شَرِّ

38 | P a g e

الشَّيْطَانِ وَشِرْكِهِ وَأَنْ أَقْتَرِفَ عَلَى نَفْسِي سُوءًا أَوْ أَجُرَّهُ إِلَى
مُسْلِمٍ

"O Allāh! Creator of the heavens and the earth, Who knows the unseen and the seen, Lord and Possessor of everything. I testify that there is none has the right to be worshiped but You; I seek refuge in You from the evil within myself, from the evil of the Shayṭān, and his (incitement to) attributing partners (to Allāh). And that we commit sin for ourselves or drag it to a Muslim."

So, one seeks refuge from the evil, its source, and its result, saying: "**the evil within myself, from the evil of the Shayṭān, and his (incitement to) attributing partners (to Allāh).**" This is seeking refuge from the cause of evil: the evil self, the cursed Shayṭān, and the result of evil.

Ibn Abbas (رَضِيَ اللهُ عَنْهُمَا) was told, "The Jews said the Shayṭān does not come to them when performing prayers, no whispers, no outside thoughts come to their mind. He said, "what does the Shayṭān do with a dead heart?" The dead heart is a closed case; Shayṭān tries his best to whisper to the living and faithful heart. Thus, one always need to strive against

Shayṭān and to seek refuge in Allāh from the evil of
the Shayṭān. Allāh (سُبْحَانَهُوَتَعَالَى) says,

$$\text{﴿ وَٱلَّذِينَ جَٰهَدُواْ فِينَا لَنَهْدِيَنَّهُمْ سُبُلَنَا ۚ وَإِنَّ ٱللَّهَ لَمَعَ ٱلْمُحْسِنِينَ ۝ ﴾}$$

**"As for those who strives hard in Us (Our
Cause), We will surely guide them to Our
Paths (i.e. Allāh's religion – Islamic
Monotheism). And verily, Allāh is with the
Muhsinīn (good-doers)."** [*Sūrah Al-Ankabut* 29:
69].

The scholars mentioned many benefits of the
remembrance of Allāh to achieve the restfulness of
the heart. Ibn Al-Qayyim authored a book entitled
*"Al-Wābil As-Sayyib"* on this subject, and it should be
kept and read. *"Al-Wābil As-Sayyib"* means the useful
rain. This book has many important benefits: It states
the benefits of remembrance. He (رَحِمَهُٱللَّهُ) mentioned
more than seventy benefits. When you read these
important benefits, you will keep closer to Allāh and
will be committed to the remembrance of Allāh
(سُبْحَانَهُوَتَعَالَى).

Of these benefits, he said:

*"Remembrance of Allāh unites the disunited and disunite the United."*

This is one of the benefits of the remembrance of Allāh. The heart requires the presence of various elements that affect its restfulness that is only obtainable through the remembrance of Allāh. In contrast, remembrance disunites the diseases filling the heart such as sadness, distress, lusts and suspicions. These diseases cannot be dispelled except with the remembrance of Allāh (سُبْحَانَهُ وَتَعَالَى).

When heart feels restful, and at ease by the remembrance of Allāh, all organs of the body feel restful and willfully perform good deeds. The Prophet (صَلَّى اللَّهُ عَلَيْهِ وَسَلَّمَ) said in authentic Ḥadīth:

أَلَا وَإِنَّ فِي الْجَسَدِ مُضْغَةً إِذَا صَلَحَتْ صَلَحَ الْجَسَدُ كُلُّهُ وَإِذَا
فَسَدَتْ فَسَدَ الْجَسَدُ كُلُّهُ أَلَا وَهِيَ الْقَلْبُ

**"Beware! There is a piece of flesh in the body if it becomes good (reformed), the whole body becomes good, but if it gets spoilt, the whole gets spoilt; and that is the heart."**

One came to Al-Hasan Al-Basrī and said:

*"I feel my heart merciless, what can I do for solving this problem? He said, 'you should make it turn away by the remembrance of Allāh.'*

Meaning: remember Allāh a lot so that this mercilessness will be removed.

Let's finish our talk with a great benefit: Allāh (سُبْحَانَهُوَتَعَالَى) said in the Noble Ḥadīth:

أَنَا مَعَ عَبْدِي مَا ذَكَرَنِي وَتَحَرَّكَتْ بِي شَفَتَاهُ

**"I am with my servant when he remembers Me and his lips move with My mention."**

So, one who remembers Allāh is honorably closer to Him (سُبْحَانَهُوَتَعَالَى).

Also, Allāh is generally with us through Allāh's knowledge as indicated in the verse:

﴾ إِلَّا هُوَ مَعَهُمْ أَيْنَ مَا كَانُوٓاْ ﴿

**"But He is with them (with His Knowledge), wherever they may be."** [*Sūrah Al-Mujadilah* 58:7]

Allāh says:

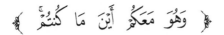

﴿ وَهُوَ مَعَكُمْ أَيْنَ مَا كُنتُمْ ﴾

**"And He is with you (by His Knowledge)
wherever you may be."** [*Sūrah Al-Hadid* 57: 4]

Allāh is specifically with some people through His
sustenance, care, giving success. To secure this status,
one should particularly commit to the remembrance
of Allāh (سُبْحَانَهُوَتَعَالَى). Allāh (سُبْحَانَهُوَتَعَالَى) says:

أَنَا مَعَ عَبْدِي مَا ذَكَرَنِي وَتَحَرَّكَتْ بِي شَفَتَاهُ

**"I am with my servant when he remembers Me
and his lips move with My mention."**

When Allāh was with the servant, his life will become
happy, and he shall lead a good life.

﴿ أَلَيْسَ ٱللَّهُ بِكَافٍ عَبْدَهُۥ ﴾

**"Is not Allāh Sufficient for His slave?"** [*Sūrah
Az-Zumar* 39:36]

If Allāh is with His servant, no evil will afflict him,
and he will be protected, blessed in the worldly life
and the Hereafter because Allāh (سُبْحَانَهُوَتَعَالَى) is with
him.

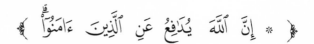

**"Truly, Allāh defends those who believe."**
[*Sūrah Al-Hajj* 22:38]

These were some reflections on Allāh's verse:

**"Verily, in the remembrance of Allāh do the hearts find rest."**

We ask Allāh with His beautiful Names and Most High attributes, and we call upon Allāh with every Name of Him with which He has described Himself, or which He has revealed in His Book, or He has taught to anyone of His creatures, or which He has chosen to keep in the knowledge of the unseen with Him to make our hearts full of the remembrance of Allāh (سُبْحَانَهُوَتَعَالَى) and to set our matters right. O Allāh! Set right our religion by virtue of which my affairs are protected, set right for me my world where my life exists, make good for me my Hereafter which is my resort to which I have to return, and make my life prone to perform all types of good, and make death a comfort for me from every evil. O Allāh! We seek refuge in You from the evil of ourselves and our bad deeds. O Allāh! We seek refuge in You from the evil of the Shayṭān and his encouragement to associate others (with You). We beseech You to guide us to the Straight Path and to guide us to every goodness and to make us one of the pious who listens to the Word [good advice] and follows it in the best manner.

Allāh knows best, and may prayers and blessings be upon his servant and Messenger Our Prophet Muḥammad, all his family and his companions.

These are some lines about the benefits of the remembrance of Allāh compiled by Shaykh Abdur Rahman Ibn Sʿadī (رَحِمَهُ ٱللَّهُ), who says:

| | |
|---|---|
| فَـذِكْرُ إِلٰهِ الْعَـرْشِ سِرًّا وَمُعْلَنًـا | يُزِيلُ الشَّقَا وَالهَمَّ عَنْكَ وَيَطْـرُدُ |
| وَيَجْلِبُ لِلْخَيْرَاتِ دُنْيَـا وَآجِـلًا | وَإِنْ يَأْتِكَ الْوَسْوَاسُ يَوْمًا يُشَـرِّدُ |
| فَقَدْ أَخْبَرَ الْمُخْتَارُ يَوْمًا لِصَحْبِهِ | بِأَنَّ كَثِيرَ الذِّكْرِ فِي السَّبْقِ مُفْـرِدُ |
| وَوَصَّى مُعَـاذًا يَسْـتَعِينُ إِلٰـهَهُ | عَلَى ذِكْرِهِ وَالشُّكْرِ بِالْحُسْنِ يَعْبُدُ |
| وَأَوْصَى لِشَخْصٍ قَدْ أَتَى لِنَصِيحَةٍ | وَقَدْ كَانَ فِي حَمْلِ الشَّـرَائِعِ يَجْهَدُ |
| بِأَنْ لَا يَزَلْ رَطْبًا لِسَـانُكَ هٰـذِهِ | تُعِـينُ عَلَى كُلِّ الْأُمُـورِ وَتُسْـعِدُ |

بِجَنَّاتِ عَدْنٍ وَالمَسَاكِنُ تُمْهَدُ وَأَخْبَرَ أَنَّ الذِّكْرَ غَرْسٌ لِأَهْلِهِ

وَمَعْهُ عَلَى كُلِّ الأُمُورِ يُسَدَّدُ وَأَخْبَرَ أَنَّ اللهَ يَـذْكُرُ عَبْـدَهُ

وَيَنْقَطِعُ التَّكْلِيفُ حِينَ يُخَلَّدُوا وَأَخْبَرَ أَنَّ الذِّكْـرَ يَـبْقَى بِجَنَّـةٍ

طَرِيـقٌ إِلَى حُبِّ الإِلَهِ وَمُرْشِـدُ وَلَوْ لَمْ يَكُنْ فِي ذِكْرِهِ غَيْرَ أَنَّهُ

وَعَنْ كُلِّ قَوْلٍ لِلدِّيَانَةِ مُفْسِـدُ وَيَنْهَى الفَتَى عَنْ غِيبَةٍ وَنَمِيمَةٍ

بِكَثْرَةِ ذِكْرِ اللهِ نِعْمَ المُوَحَّدُ لَكَانَ لَنَا حَظٌّ عَظِيمٌ وَرَغْبَةٌ

كَمَا قَلَّ مِنَّا لِلْإِلَهِ التَّعَبُّدُ وَلَكِنَّنَا مِنْ جَهْلِنَا قَلَّ ذِكْرُنَا

*Remembering Allāh privately and publicly*

*Removes sadness and distress,*

*Bestows good matter in this worldly life and the Hereafter.*

*And will scatter whispering if it comes to you.*

*And the Prophet told his companions*

*That remembering a lot make one have gone ahead.*

*And advised Mu'ādh to seek Allāh's help*

*To remember, praise and worship well.*

*And advised someone who sought advice*

*While he feels acts of worship are too weary*

*That his tongue should be kept with the remembrance
of Allāh.*

*This helps make matters and make one happy.*

*And told that remembrance is a fertile land*

*For Eden paradise and beautiful mansions.*

*And told that Allāh mentions his servant*

*And with His slave, everything will be set right.*

*And told that remembrance will be in paradise,*

*While there is no acts of worship ordained.*

*And if there is no benefit in remembrance but*

*It is a way and a guide to love Allāh.*

*And forbids doing acts of backbite and gossip*

*And every saying misuse religion.*

*We will have a great luck and desire*

*With remembering Allāh a lot, none has the right to be worshiped but He.*

*But our ignorance make us remember Allāh very few,*

*And worship Allāh very few.*

These are great lines concerning the benefits of the remembrance of Allāh. All that is mentioned in these lines based on evidence from the Noble Qur'ān and the Sunnah of the Prophet (ﷺ).

And Allāh knows best, and May prayers and blessings be upon our Prophet Muḥammad, his family, and his companions.

# Questions

**Question #1:** What are the best books to read concerning remembrance and supplications which are free from weak and fabricated Ḥadīths? And what are the best editions of these books?

**Answer:** The books which are compiled in this regard are a lot; there are the books of remembrance which are compiled by people of innovation in which remembrance and supplications are created by themselves or based on fabricated Ḥadīths. Muslim should not be occupied with this remembrance, but we should remember Allāh with what is mentioned by the Prophet (ﷺ).

Thus, Muslim should choose the books by the renowned scholars and who care for the Ḥadīth of the Prophet (ﷺ) to benefit from. Fortunately, there are many printed and published books that can be read by the Muslim, such as the book entitled "*Al-Wābil As-Sayyib*" by Ibn Al-Qayyim (رحمه الله), and the book of Shaykh Al-Islam "*Al-Kalim At-Tayyib,*" and "*Tuhfatul Akhyar*" by Shaykh Abdul Aziz Ibn Baz. (رحمه الله).

SHAYKH 'ABDUR-RAZZĀQ IBN 'ABDUL-MUHSIN AL-'ABBĀD AL-BADR

There are many books based on the authentic Hadīth of the Prophet (ﷺ) the knowledge seeker can benefit from. However, one should keep a distance from the books that are not based on the Sunnah, particularly the ones in which deeds are specified to a certain time [inconsistent with the Sunnah] and remembrances inconsistent with the Noble Qur'ān and the Sunnah of the Prophet (ﷺ).

Sometimes, laypeople publish papers in which there are particular remembrances and supplications, saying whoever mentioned it would be protected, gain something, and lose something. They invented many benefits without any evidence. So, the Muslim should not pay attention to this or rely upon it.

**Question #2:** If this supplication for distress is said once, but I still feel distressed, can I repeat it?

It is authentic in the Prophetic Sunnah that this supplication is said in the morning and the evening?

**Answer:** This supplication is not one of the morning and evening remembrances. If this supplication is said, Allāh will make the sadness, distress, and anxiety go away. So, one should be committed to this supplication. It is important to think about its meaning and to reflect upon its significance so that it will have a great effect. If one is afflicted with sadness and distress, he should repeat this supplication. This supplication is a resort to Allāh, submission to Him and calling upon Him (سُبْحَانَهُوَتَعَالَى). So, this supplication should be mentioned again and again if sadness and distress are repeated.

**Question #3:** Is the Ḥadīth of (nothing averts the Divine Decree but supplication) an authentic Ḥadīth? Can the Divine Decree be averted?

**Answer:** This Ḥadīth is mentioned by the Prophet (صَلَّى اللَّهُ عَلَيْهِ وَسَلَّمَ)

لَا يَرُدُّ الْقَدَرَ إِلَّا الدُّعَاء

**"Nothing averts the Divine Decree but supplication."**

Supplication is associated with the Divine Decree. This is the meaning of this Ḥadīth. This means that if one is decreed to get in trouble or so, and he prays for Allāh (سُبْحَانَهُوَتَعَالَى) to avert this trouble, all this is written in the Preserved Tablet.

﴿ وَكُلُّ شَىْءٍ فَعَلُوهُ فِى ٱلزُّبُرِ ۝ وَكُلُّ صَغِيرٍ وَكَبِيرٍ مُّسْتَطَرٌ ۝ ﴾

"And everything they have done is noted in (their) Records (of deeds). And everything, small and big, is written down (in Al-Lauh Al-Mahfuz already beforehand i.e. before it befalls, or is done by its doer)." [*Sūrah Al-Qamar* 54:52-53]

**Question #4:** The Hadīth of,

مَنْ قَال لَا إِلَهَ إِلَّا اللهُ وَحْدَهُ لَا شَرِيكَ لَهُ الْمُلْكُ وَ لَهُ الْحَمْدُ وَ هُوَ

عَلَى كُلِّ شَيْءٍ قَدِيرٌ فِي يَوْمٍ مِائَةَ مَرَّةٍ كَانَ لَهُ حِرْزٌ مِنَ الشَّيْطَانِ

"Whoever says [the following] hundred times in the morning will be guarded against the Shaytān: 'none has the right to be worshiped but Allāh Alone, no partners with Him, to Him belongs the Bounty, to Him belongs the Praise, He is Able to do all things."

Should it be said hundred times the whole day? Or hundred times in the morning and hundred times in the evening?

**Answer:** What I remember that this Hadīth of,

مَنْ قَالَ لَا إِلَهَ إِلَّا اللَّهُ وَحْدَهُ لَا شَرِيكَ لَهُ لَهُ الْمُلْكُ وَلَهُ الْحَمْدُ
وَهُوَ عَلَى كُلِّ شَيْءٍ قَدِيرٌ فِي يَوْمٍ مِائَةَ مَرَّةٍ

"Whoever says none has the right to be worshiped but Allāh Alone, no partners with Him, to Him belongs the Bounty, to Him belongs the Praise, He is Able to do all things hundred times a day."

The other Ḥadīth mentions hundred times in the morning and the evening:

مَنْ قَالَ حِينَ يُصْبِحُ وَحِينَ يُمْسِي سُبْحَانَ اللَّهِ وَبِحَمْدِهِ مِائَةَ مَرَّةٍ
لَمْ يَأْتِ أَحَدٌ يَوْمَ الْقِيَامَةِ بِأَفْضَلَ مِمَّا جَاءَ بِهِ إِلَّا أَحَدٌ قَالَ مِثْلَ
مَا قَالَ أَوْ زَادَ عَلَيْهِ

"He who recites in the morning and the evening the statement: "Glory be to Allāh" one hundred times, will not be surpassed on the Day of Resurrection by anyone with better deeds than one who utters the same words or utters more of these words."

This Ḥadīth is authentic, and this supplication should be said in the morning and the evening.

**Question #5:** One asks about a book entitled "Fiqh of Al-Adkār and supplications;" is the compiler of this book published the other part of it?

**Answer:** What I know is that the second part is about to be printed in shaa Allāh. May Allāh make it easy to be printed and benefited from.

**Question #6:** What is the meaning of remembrance of Allāh inside one's heart?

**Answer:** Ibn Al-Qayyim said in his book entitled "Al-Wābil As-Sayyib" that remembrance of Allāh is divided into two types: remembrance of Allāh by the heart and by the tongue. Remembrance of Allāh (سُبْحَانَهُوَتَعَالَى) by the heart means glorifying and loving Allāh, remembering His Grandeur and His Names and Attributes. Remembrance of Allāh by tongue indicates glorifying (saying Subhānallāh), praising (saying Al-Hamdulillah), Tahlil (saying La ilaha illa Allāh), Takbir (saying Allahu Akbar) and recitation of the Qur'ān; all this is a remembrance of Allāh.

Remembrance of Allāh may be of the heart and tongue, and the best is to remember Allāh by both, tongue and heart.

Allāh Knows best, and prayers and blessings be upon our Prophet Muḥammad, his family, and his companions.

Made in the USA
Middletown, DE
13 July 2021

44036205R00033